I was born in th |
in the sixties – ?   , ̣ʳ
Lourdes, and <u>my</u> life began in the
seventies.....and eighties in Farnworth –
Nowadays it's the only place you can go
within a 20 mile radius – and still be at the
scene of a crime.

So why am I writing this book ?? Good
question, Probably its because my kids who
are now fully grown with their own children,
and are sick to death of hearing my
repetitive stories about - 'In my days.'

I can only apologise profoundly if you are
offended by some of the language I have
used, although I have tried to tone it down
some. It is what it is – and those were the
words used in the 70' & 80's. Nothing much
different from the bad language used today,
except today, no one cares who it offends.

It would be pointless me writing a book,
based on this era, of skinheads, gang fights,
territory wars and general adolescents if I

1

had to replace some of the 'blue' words with more select adjectives like 'golly gosh', 'oh dear' or even 'silly billy'

Most of the characters in my book are 'real' some of the names have been changed – for obvious reasons – and because I don't want a lynch mob outside my house.

I'm hoping that everyone who reads this book find they can relate or recognise some of the characters from their own personal friends and acquaintances.

I've tried to write down truthful events to the best of my knowledge, as my slowly decreasing memory bank will allow.

Most of the times I was present, other times when I wasn't I'm happy with the facts given to me by my trusted friends who were.

Okay, maybe one or two hemlines have be lengthened, and some shortened, I've added a bit of 'extra' drama, or predicament to some chapters, and I've also had to extract some 'heavy' or discriminating facts in some of the stories, But, I'll let you make your own mind up which is fact or which is fiction ?

I've been asked several times about the title 'Bag of Nails' – Each nail in the bag is compared to the many people I have met and shared, and still share my life with, Imagine a bag of nails, all lengths and sizes, some big and strong and holding together heavy structures, some rusty and bent, some small but handy to have around, Some past their use and thrown away, Some not trusted to hold anything together, some nailed together to construct a formation and still holding it together after many years, Some lost forever or used in new formations or elements, I hope you can understand and compare similarity to this with people you have met throughout your life. I believe 'everyone' has their own 'bag of nails'

I Hope you enjoy reading it.

I enjoyed writing it.

BAG OF NAILS

TOMMY 'B'

Tommy stood at the bus station waiting for the dusty old number 14 to pull in, Eventually, late as usual, the big red bus pulled in. Tommy scanned the passengers as they got off like an hungry wolf. The bus minutes later pulled away. 'Bitch' he said to himself. Lynne hadn't come.

 12 long months living at her majesty's pleasure, he touched the top pocket of his crombie overcoat – his supply of Durex would be redundant tonight...unless, he got lucky. Walking through the arcade 'wary' he headed for the nearest watering hole – The Market Inn, the place was busy, he saw familiar faces and headed for the bar counter 'Pint of lager love' he said as he mentally MRI scanned the busy hive.

'Oi! ..wait your fuckin turn mate' said a steroid fuelled, pea head, as he looked at Tommy with challenging eyes. 'Don't just walk in, and think you own the fuckin place' Tommy showing no interest in this outburst and calmly looked away. 'I'm talking to you dickhead' said the pea head, Still no response from Tommy, this guy wanted aggro, Tommy just wanted a pint.

Pea Head was surrounded by 'Blondie' lookalike wannabees, watching his every move. Pea head now got closer, just a few inches away, from Tommy's unaffected stance – Big mistake – he reached out to grab Tommy's coat ..'I'm fucking talking to you, you ignorant twat ! Do you know who i am ? He obviously didn't know who 'Tommy' was or my guess would be, he would have gone running for the hills. Within a split second Tommy had spun round and performed the perfect 'Bolton' handshake smack down on pea heads rasping coke distorted face.

 Pea head dropped to the sticky beer soaked carpet like a ton of bricks. 'You broke my nose you fucking cunt !! he said blood streaming down his punch drunk face. Tommy turned back round to the bar counter, looked at the chunky tattooed barmaid 'You done that pint yet ? he said.

The Blondie 'hanger onners' had now separated from their pack – all but one....

'Hi, Tommy – It's been a while' she said, Tommy nodded, maybe the pack of three wouldn't be redundant tonight after all – and beggars can't be choosers.

Tommy woke up the following morning, the rancid stench of tobacco, stale beer and dirty knickers filled his nostrils, he heaved, didn't know what was the worse smell – that or the vile wafts of semen, piss and dried blood he'd exhaled every morning in Strangeways Prison.

He looked down at the grubby stained sheets, his nights conquest was lying there, comatose with weed, snake bite and who gives a fuck.....Tommy left.

ROBBIE

Robbie's bright piercing eyes scoured the dance floor, Illuminous blue, carefully x-raying each potential female, looking far beyond the halter neck top or the Chelsea girl midi dress, Robbie imagined what was underneath. The club was full, Friday night, payday, everyone fuelled up on cherry B and cider or lager with a blackcurrant top. Julie leaned against the staging near the D.J box, Robbie had seen her before in 'The Well' – she looked like a fish out of water, quiet and shy, trying to disguise the fact that she had, had a bit more to drink than she was used to.

Giving himself a quick once over in the mirrored wall, he smiled at his reflection, confident that his light blue wranglers, checked 'Ben Sherman' shirt and beloved black polished 'Royals' were the business. Yes Robbie looked good, he always did,

Robbie loved the Drifters and he would often use their songs as chat up-lines for a potential quick 'wham bam thank you mam' he would often stand in the Doorway of Woolworths on Market Street, and any passing girl that took his eye he would unashamedly belt out '' Little girl you look so lonely, I see you are feeling blue, Aint no use in staying at home – I know what youuu should dooo...Come on over to my place..'' Sometime – it worked – sometimes it didn't.

Julie was different, she wasn't like the other Saturday night conquests, she had class. The only man she would ever run after – would be the ice cream man.

Robbie sashayed over to were Julie was standing 'Alright' he asked her. His eyes looking straight forward – stay cool Robbie stay cool. Julie nodded back. The next ten minutes were spent both of them standing there like two exhibits from Madame Tussauds.

Robbie held out his half filled glass of flat warm Fosters 'Want a drink of this' he said. Julie declined his generous offer with another nod of her head and a look that said she was only seconds away from spewing her guts. James Browns sex machine blasted out from the D.J box. ' You going Tommys flat after here ? his mums away at his sisters for the night so we are all heading up there' Robbie asked and with the enthusiasm of someone waiting on death row.

Julie shrugged her shoulders. 'O.K might see you there then' he said..He was certain that 'last' shrug of her shoulders was a 'come on'.

Ahhh Robbie, loved his women almost as much as he loved himself, always smartly dressed, painter and decorator, always had a bob or two in his wallet, not a bad catch except he didn't have much going on upstairs, he was as thick as pig shit.

That night at Tommy's flat, he made his claim on Julie, he spent the next day strutting round like a peacock on amphetamine, Robbie was Julies 'First' what an achievement, he bragged to anyone who would listen that he'd bedded a virgin and had popped her cherry , what a guy. The only thing that made that night a magical fairytale – was that Robbie had two ugly sisters.

When Julie heard about this she wasn't too happy, so she decided to tell everyone her version, about the event, when, half way through, Julie had to inform the 'sex machine' Robbie that she was still wearing her tights ! Nice one Julie – Men wear the pants – but us girls control the zipper..

They stayed as a couple for almost two years, then as young love does it dwindled away Julie went on to become an Butchers wife, and Robbie..well he just went on being Robbie.

Sadly Robbie passed away several years ago, but whenever I pass Woolworths these days I can mentally hear and see Robbie, hands in his pockets, shirt collar turned up, and his smooth vocal attempts at his version of.... 'Come on over to my place'.

PETE

Pete was Tommys best mate, and he had a younger brother, Brad, he was the joker, the wind-up merchant, his buddy was David – one of the 'brothers', between them they would keep our 'lot' amused with their 'unfunny jokes' and slap dash comments always prepared to 'wind-up' anyone gullible enough to believe anything they said they took no prisoners – You were either 'at the table' or 'on the menu' with them two.

 Pete and Tommy, shared everything together, from a 'borrowed' car, the local slapper, or a social club's easy to break into cigarette machines. They even shared a few 'free' holidays in the local remand centres or prisons.

Pete was a good catholic educated lad, religiously went to confession Friday night, and mass on a Sunday. The proverbial good son, who would help little old ladies across the road (whether they wanted to cross or not). Pete had, his 'Alter ego' to keep him amused.

Nothing in life affected him, he wasn't scared of the devil – he danced with him ! If you did Pete wrong you had one chance – it was called 'not a fucking cat in hells chance'.

Human error had no place in Pete's vocabulary, he had no filter, and he didn't feel the pain of his enemies screams or loss of body parts.

There was one time Pete was on a week release from one of his stints in 'Strangeways' he was allowed home for a week to try to adjust before his permanent release in 4 weeks time, he'd called into the White Horse for a pint and a game of brag with a few of his bakery working buddies. In walked 'Ferret' ...'Alright Pete mate, nice to see you, looking good pal, bending for that soap in the showers has been good to you..' he said, looking around at the faces of the bakery guys for a burst of applause or even a snide smirk.....he received silence, even the dog that was lay at the side of the bar silently skulked over to a safer area.

Pete didn't need to answer – just one look from his dark grey narrowed eyes said it all...' Ferret turned green, and nervously laughing said 'Only joking buddy, don't mean anything, just joking that's all' Pete turned back round to his game, he was doing O.K, long empty days in the nick playing brag with his fellow inmates had proved to be profitable today, he was 100 quid up.

Like a sewer rat, Ferret let the dust settle for a while, before he approached Pete at the card table, 'here you are matey, no hard feelings, got a bit of nice gear you might be interested in'.

Ferret, pulled a box from under his scruffy brown anorak, Pete glanced over. Opening the tatty box he pulled out a wristwatch. ' Top quality this, a real genuine Rolex- not your crappy market stuff ' he handed over the timepiece to Pete, 'A mate of mine got it from an house he was fitting a kitchen in for - silly twats left it lying about'.

What's the damage said Pete. Ferret looked around over his shoulder like a dodgy vicar in an adult book shop ' one and a half ton to you' worth at least double that '.

 Pete handed it back uninterested. 'Okay' said the Ferret, 'I'll take a ton I won't be making a penny on it but cos your a mate ....I'm telling you these beauties are selling for fuckin hundreds'

Pete looked at the columns of coins and layers of fivers on the table, he had standards, he liked quality things, he'd be going back to the nick in 2 days time, maybe it would be an investment to wear for his 'get out of jail free card' when he made his return in four weeks time. Pete handed over the cash and slipped the watch on his wrist.

IAN & WRIGHTY

Ian , small and compact, like a 'Tonka toy' the girls used to think he was 'cute', ..Not only was he cute – he could have been a Michael Angelo of the eighties, a brilliant artist and – forger, he worked for a local printers.

It wasn't long before Ian's artistic talent emerged in conversation amongst the lads and, it was decided , a bit extra cash would come in handy, and it was decided by the 'elders' that Ian was now elected to be the 'chosen one' and after careful planning and intense discussions, within a couple of weeks the 'mint' was established up and running. At first, a couple of hundred quid was printed off for a taster, but greed is a fat demon with a small mouth, whatever you feed it, is not enough, the couple of hundred soon became thousands, ninety thousand to be exact, which in the seventies, was a pretty serious amount of wonga.

The men's clothing shops in Market street, Manchester profited well by it, yes everyone had the benefit of Ian's toy cash.

Our crew were the best dressed skinheads this side of Astley Bridge.

Of course it all came crashing down like a lorry load of popped air balloons.

Saturday afternoon, the lads were sat as usual in the Market Inn watching 'Grandstand'. In walks Wrighty, a mentally challenged hanger on, who's only claim to fame ....was that he would dip his salmon paste butties in his coffee on his dinner break where he worked at the local polystyrene factory, and display his Grundy's with skid marks to anyone who unfortunately happened to be in his company.

Well, Wrighty got his hands on a couple hundred quid of these dodgy paper notes, which had to be spent to get the 'real' cash in change.

Wrighty with all his worldly wisdom had earlier decided to venture to the local 'Kwik Save' to exchange some of the fake 'tenners' for goods, he walked round the supermarket aisles, and picked himself up a packet of custard creams, costing 12 pence, ...paying for them with a tenner, the little trainee cashier gave him his 9.88 pence change.

By now well chuffed with himself, the little plastic gangster decided to repeat his party trick again..and again ..and again – 9 times to be exact – all with the same cashier, Now the till girl became just a little bit suspicious of this, also noticing that the fake tenners ALL had the same serial numbers..and so with the push of a button, security was called and...so was the dibble.

Wrighty was taken to the local cop shop and charged – and here he was in the Market Inn after being released on bail, now telling his story.

He'd be telling this story to his grandkids one day in the future he thought to himself, -

money without brains, is always dangerous..
.... 100,000 sperm – and he was the fastest
!!!

Obviously the lads in the 'Market' became
nervous and had no choice but to believe
Wrighty when he said he hadn't stitched
anyone up or mentioned names.

I was at Tommys flat that night when we
heard about it, Robbie came round and
spilled the news.

Me and Tommy were sat by the coal fire on
the couch, and so giving each other a
knowing glance , we knew what we had to
do.

There was about 35 grand on the top of the
fireplace, it broke my heart, watching the
cash disappear into black flakes of
nothingness as it burned on Tommys coal
fire. We knew that Tommy would be the first
call, on the old bills list.

Farnworth cops watched Tommy's every
move, they wanted him in them cells so bad,
give him the mattress treatment, like they

had done to so many others.(The mattress was used in the cells, and a few of these upstanding, respected public serving officers would cover it over anyone they had took a disliking to when they'd been arrested, then they would have their fun kicking and smacking seven shades of shit out of their victim. The mattress stopped their boot marks and truncheons giving any recognisable markings on the victim's body).

Don't forget this was the seventies !

Over the weeks there were house calls, statements, alibis etc..luckily no one was pin pointed, except Wrighty, who got 6 months in Risley Remand. I remember the headlines in the Bolton Evening News ' Police bust local forgery operation' fortunately Wrighty kept his mouth shut no else one got busted.

To Ian's credit..it also mentioned in the same article that Scotland yard had made a statement saying that the bank notes were the best forgeries they had ever seen, high five Ian !

THE BROTHERS

The Brothers, I'll call them Dave and Brian,
As for sibling similarities ?? No two brothers
could ever be more personality opposites
than if they had both been conceived in two
different continents.

Dave was a kind, caring lad, who would give
you everything he possessed – if you needed
it..Brian would take everything you had – if
HE needed it.

Both brothers were close and although their
personalities created constant arguments
with each other, they always stuck up for
each other when needed.

 Brought up in an household by a lovely but,
brow beaten mother who had no choice, in
them days, but to adhere to a hard, heavy
drinking, gambling, lazy wife beater.

Dave loved being with the crew, he felt like
he belonged, everyone liked him, trusted
him.

When the local neighbouring rival town gangs had their battles he often relied on his brothers 'tough guy' status to use when he got himself in trouble with the 'hard men' from Little Hulton or Swinton. 'Brian *****'s my brother' he'd say..some of the rivals would back off – sometimes they didn't give a toss who his brother was – and he'd get a good hammering. He didn't care... Dave was one of the lads.

And Brian??, he was nothing special to look at, but he had this weird charismatic charm that could hypnotise the belly warmers off any girl - and he did very often !..Soft grey soppy 'puppy dog' eyes and a cheeky grin.

He was a steady member of the crew, always there when his mates needed him, handy lad, even more handy when some of the lads and their girlfriends where having a bad patch – Brian always made sure the girls kept a smile on their face, how no one ever found out about his booty calls I'll never know. Brian could pick pockets better than any 'Fagin' he would often buy his mates a pint, with the cash he'd lifted from their pockets –

Good old Brian. He got his exercise from –
pushing his luck.

Nowadays, I can take a walk around
Farnworth and often, recognise, similarities
in adults and their kids, same grey puppy
eyes, same cheeky grin – Ohh yes he
certainly got about did our Brian. Sewing his
wild oats with a condom wasn't an option.
Brian had no boundaries.

NELLY

Nelly was, and still is one of my best buddies, she had crystal blue eyes, pink rosy cheeks, sharp turned up nose, blonde hair, she was and still is stunning.

We spent many a Saturday afternoon trundling around the shops in Manchester, Werfs, Chelsea Girl, Bus Stop, 2001, Oasis underground Market, never leaving until we had only our bus fare home left.

I had a fabulous job, I worked at G.U.S catalogue Office in Bolton, great pay for the seventies, and Nelly's Parents were pretty well off so we always had a few bob to spend, and we certainly knew how to spend it.

Every 3 or 4 weeks, we'd visit our friends 'Mark and Gerald' they had a hairdressing salon there, in the centre of Manchester called 'Harvey and Ruperts' and, on leaving with our 'Vidal Sassoon' hairstyles, we would make our last call before the bus home - Derbas shoe shop. Derbas were the suppliers of the most fantastic, outrageous footwear, nowadays it would be on par with the 'Gucci' or 'Valentino's'. We bought shoes like they were chocolate bars, I bought a pair of black patent leather, 4 inch sole 6 inch block heel, ankle straps, Nelly bought them in Burgundy, they were expensive 25.00 a big wad of cash forty years ago, We didn't blink an eye it was only money.

God forbid if me or Nelly ever bought shoes from Timpsons or Barrats - No not our style...something we had in abundance, style.

Friday nights we'd get ready for 'our' club – 'Troggs' a.k.a 'Big Apple' a.k.a Splinters...and thats were we'd throw some shapes to the sounds of 'Smarty Pants', 'You can do magic' and 'Floyd Joy'...'Love on a Mountain Top', I'm stone in Love with You'.... the list goes on and on.

We both loved Northern Soul – but Tamla Motown flowed in our blood, and still does to this day.

If no one offered us epilepsy medication after we'd done on the dance floor, we would consider it a victory.

We spent many a Friday night sat on the empty Market stalls , drinking Bulmers Cider and Cherry 'B'.

One of the weirdest things we used to do was, buy a small Blackpool roll (bread) and a quarter of Luncheon meat, to eat from 'Millies' corner shop on Peel street, before we binged on the drink, this would soak up the alcohol.

Troggs entrance was at the top of a long flight of stairs, Believe me, a week never went by without one of us plummeting down in our 'Derba' heels, but we were pissed and didn't feel much – until the morning.

 We always had our 'boyfriends' to walk – or usually carry us home, Nelly, with Brad – me with Tommy.

THE WAY WE WERE

There were so many styles in the seventies and eighties, midis, maxis, halter neck dresses, and the biggest false eyelashes you could manage, great for weekend clubbing, then for a more dressed down day attire Harrington jackets, Cheesecloth shirts, wide bottomed jeans.

One of the most prominent styles were the skinhead dress, The lads wore short 'Levi' drainpipe jeans, Ben Sherman or Fred Perry Short sleeved shirts and braces, completing the look with high leg 'ox blood' highly polished doc marten boots, and a splash of Brut aftershave. The girls wore Mexican peasant blouses, wide bottomed pants, frayed jeans, military or denim jackets. Towards the end of the 70's early 80's, the drainpipe jeans and braces etc were gradually being replaced with extra wide legged two-tone trousers with 4 inch waistbands, Black knee length 'Crombie' overcoats, each top pocket held a cotton handkerchief, 'Ice blue', for Farnworth, and 'Red' for Bolton and Little Hulton, these were paired up with matching socks of the same colour.

The two-tone trousers played a major role for the wigan casino 'Northern Soul' all nighters, worn with black polished leather bottomed 'Royals'. They wafted round like yacht sails when the soul spins were performed on the dance floor.

The girls wore pretty much the same crombies, check shirt, even wearing mens 'Royal' shoes, or 'monkey boots' most of the girls wore their hair in a 'feather cut' style, thinly layered and long sides and an ultra short blunt fringe – 'original he-she's' Bloodywell frightens me now thinking about it !

WIGAN CASINO

I only have to hear 'Al Wilsons' The Snake – and I'm transported back to Wigan Pier, and our Northern Soul dance moves. The sweat on a Saturday night on the dance floor alone would have filled a small reservoir.

If you liked Northern Soul – as nearly everyone did then, Wigan Casino was the place to be seen, rammed packed every Saturday night, we'd get the train down from Bolton, then we'd congregate in a room over the top of the Casino, in a 'make-shift' cafe style setting, swapping and selling rare single records,' Chairman of the Board', 'Landslide' – 'Do I love You' by Frankie Wilson – and Wayne Gibson's 'Under my Thumb' all timeless music memories.

Some of us would buy or swap the more recreational substance, - 'Speed' - Blueies, Duramin, Tenuate Dospan, Double parrellis, and good old Pondrax....all of them ' gotta haves' if you wanted to last the night in the casino.

Tommy or Brad didn't go to the Casino, me and Nelly would go with some of the others in our group.

Them two were more interested in 'Elton Johns' 'Saturday nights all right for fighting' – and they would do just that !....almost every Saturday night in Farnworth...with 'intruding' gangs from neighbouring towns. One particular visitor from Little Hulton, was called Asunta ...'Sunny' for short...18 stone solid, skinhead, built like a brick shithouse, no morals no filter and no fucking conscience....Sunny was somebody to be reckoned with, Sunny never fought one on one, where was the fun in that ? No, Sunny fought 2-3 and sometimes more – ending up usually with the rivals flat out, broken nose, spitting blood, rolling in pain – Not bad for a 23 year old WOMAN ! yes Sunny was a fully fledged female, who made it very clear that she enjoyed the company of other females.

On lazy Sunny afternoons we'd all congregate in the Market place, we called it 'The Warry'- havn't a clue why ? We'd sit there chatting, swigging cans of Heinekin, and soaking up the heat – and believe me we had proper summer heat in the seventies We would stroll into 'Birches' cafe for a pastie, or nip across the road to the 'Chicken Barbeque' for a chicken and stuffing barm... best stuffing I ever tasted.

Sometimes, Troggs resident D.J Billy Wood, -' Woody' share a couple of cheeky spliffs with us, he used to wear a long cream suede coat, trimmed with sheepskin, white grandfather vest and hippy beads fastened around his neck and wrists. He eventually moved away to Newquay, as did many of the 'Farnworth Lot' – Some stayed for a couple of weeks, some stayed the summer season, some stayed and made their home there – as Woody did. All working at the many hotels there as barmen, cooks, chambermaids – there was work for everyone.

Farnworth was always an hard place to leave, but sometimes, you have to turn around, give a smile, throw the match, and burn that fucking bridge.

DEBS & KAREN

Deb was one of the girls, worked with Nelly at the hairdressers for a while, she was slightly built with shiny black, curly hair, she was a 'Fence sitter' never got involved in any of our girly squabbles. She dizzily plodded on day to day, nothing fazed her, placid and kind and an ardent fan of the Northern Soul scene.

She lived with her Mum and Dad, at the local 'off-licence'... now THATS what I'm talking about – it was like Christmas every week for us, Deb's Mum and Dad would spend their Saturday night and Sunday away at their friends house – leaving Debs with a 'free bar' just for us – unlimited amounts of alcohol – We'd sleep on the couch, the floors anywhere we could slump our 'speed' and 'liquor' consumed body masses.

Sunday morning would come round and we'd be awaken to the sound of Deb, asking who wanted a drink – Tea ?? Coffee? No ! It was an hair of the dog for us – Vodka, Whiskey or the odd toxic barley wine.

That was a real 'Sunday breakfast.

Karen was the youngest of our group. Karen didn't have a good life, her Mother was an alcoholic, regularly coming home days and nights smashed, then she'd go on beer withdrawal she would smash little Karen about the house.

She was always covered in bruises and lumps on some part of her frail frame. Even though her life was hell, she never complained to any of us, she was just glad to be part of our circle, and she clung to us and followed us everywhere like a lost sheep.

Karen was only 13, but she was mature and level headed for her age – she had to be, Yet too young to go into the local pubs, she would often sit patiently outside in all weathers smiling and waving to us through the window. Sometimes we'd sneak an half filled glass of cider and a bag of smiths out to her. Now looking back her life must of been absolute shit, but we were all young, and only interested in the opposite sex, space cakes and having fun. The lads however would use her as a stooge, they'd pick on her with their snide comments, Carry her small struggling body to the waste bin outside the Market Inn and tip her in it regularly, One night they cut a big huge chunk out of her long feathered hair and then cellotaped it above the bar – yes they were bastards – our bastards. But Karen always came back next day, unaffected, all she craved, was attention – no matter how bad it was – she felt like she belonged.

Last I heard of Karen was over 35 years ago, she had met a guy, they'd moved in together somewhere in Levenshulme, he was a 'bad un' he'd beat her regularly, the only joy in her life I was told was her baby boy – who she lived for, sadly Karen's path wasn't intended to be happy, and we heard the little boy had died from Meningitis when he was three years old.

 Some of us tried to get in contact with her, but had no luck. I just hope and pray that wherever she is today she has found some happiness in her life.

THE ROLEX

Pete stood in his parents front garden on the estate, breathing in the scent of carnations, rose bushes and dog piss, 2 days left till he would go back to the 'queens' residence – Strangeways.

'Tell your mum put kettle on Pete' said a familiar voice - it was Tommy. 'sorted pal' said Pete.

 The two went into the neat little kitchen 'Hello Mrs Patterson' said Tommy..'Hello Tommy – I'm sure you can smell that bloody kettle boiling' she replied. She liked Tommy, he was always polite and she knew he'd always have Pete's back covered, when needed - which was pretty often.

 'What's that you got on your wrist ?' said Tommy. 'Rolex watch i bought off ferret for a hundred bar – worth twenty times that mate' said Pete.

Pete handed the watch over to Tommy ' Nice bit of tack eh?' he said. Tommy examined the watch like a Neuro- surgeon.

'Snide, Pete – It's a fucking snide mate' he said. Pete's polecat eyes narrowed and he scanned Tommy's face for a smirk that would tell him he was having him on – Tommy stared back ' Its fake you daft twat – Ferrets fucked you over!

Tommy tried to explained to Pete that the second hand on a 'Kosher' Rolex 'sweeps' the second hand on a snide 'tick'. 'Fucking ferrets going to get it!' spat Pete.

So a visit down to the White Horse pub that night was arranged - to have a little 'chat' with the Ferret.

The White Horse was quiet, a few regulars stood at the bar drinking their pints of mixed. 'Ferret here ?' said Pete to the landlord. 'Not yet, usually gets in about 10' he replied. It was 8.30, Tommy and Pete, ordered their pints, sat down in their usual seats and waited like two prairie wolves.

At 10.15 doors burst open, in walks Ferret, straight to the bar ' half of bitter Malc' he said. Malc pulled a glass from the shelf, nodding in the direction of the two amigos.

Sat in the corner, ferret looked round, immediately, feeling the colour drain from his narrow pot holed face, his eyes transfixed like a rabbit caught in a cars headlights.. ' O.K Tommy, alright Pete' he said unable to hide his nervous twitch.

Pete smirked 'I'm alright, how about you Tommy, you alright?' Tommy responded ' Yeh I'm alright Pete never been better'. The two looked at each other and knowingly smirked at the tense atmosphere they had just created.

Pete nodded to Ferret indicating the empty seat at the table, grabbing his beer, ferret scuttled across and sat down. 'It's about this piece of crap, on my wrist ferret, making my wrist all red and scabby, any advice on what I should do? Said Pete. 'Err no Pete, don't know how it's done that, you might have an allergy or bad reaction to the metal' he replied 'Only fucking allergy I have is of no-mark, spineless scammers' said Pete. Ferret tried to speak but Pete held his fingers to his lips shhh...and ferret did just that.

' Now let's imagine that you really didn't have a clue the watch was snide, and you'd no intentions of ripping me off – you wouldn't do that would you Ferret? Me being such a good mate of yours' spat Pete who then looked at Tommy who was sitting flicking and lighting his zippo, oblivious of the tension veins prominent on Pete's neck and the fear ignited beads of sweat on ferrets brow. 'I'm a decent sort of bloke Ferret always prepared to give a mate the benefit of doubt', Pete now deliberately over exaggerating the word 'mate'.

Ferret sat there glass in hand his eyes never leaving Pete's.

' Tell you what – Be in here tomorrow night 8 o'clock sharp – and I mean sharp! – bring with you my hundred nicker, and let's say another couple of ponies (50 quid) just for my inconvenience and I'll consider calling it quits' said Pete. 'If you want to pull a fast one – Go chat up a cheetah - now fuck off ! Ferret scuttled from his seat, knocking his glass over, Tommy wasn't happy, some of the beer had splashed his prized 'Royals'

Ferret was traumatised Tommy didn't need to speak he just lashed out the splashed royal right in between Ferrets legs, that should dry it – Ferret fell to the ground holding his groin.

'You ready now Pete' said Tommy, 'Yes I'm sorted' Pete replied and getting up Pete poured the remains of his warm pint over Ferrets head. '8 o'clock Ferret' whispered Pete stooping down over the blubbering Ferret. They both strolled out of the pub - you could have heard a pin drop.

When the next night came – 8 o'clock, Tommy and Pat waited patiently in The White Horse, it was busier than usual, they passed the next couple of hours filling the time with a few games of Brag, .. by 10 o'clock it was obvious that Ferret wasn't going to show Silly, Silly Ferret. – Big. Big, mistake.

 Pete was going back to Strangeways in the morning – but he'd be back in four weeks.

TROGGS

Troggs was open most nights, and during the week if Nell was with Brad, I'd take myself down and have an hour with my mate Val, she worked behind the bar, and would go down early, about sevenish, before doors opened at 8.30.

We had a good few freebies from the stock, and by 8.30 I was up and giving it large by myself, on the little square dance floor, watching the early birds gradually stumble in from the streets.

It was on one of these nights I'd gone down, to Troggs, Val was nervously wiping over the bar top, shaking her head when she saw me.

My 'You alright Val? Was interrupted with a piercing scream – What the F....???, and then another scream followed by inaudible sounds from what sounded like a gang of football hooligans. 'What's going on in there' I said, nodding towards the back room office. 'Don't ask' said Val ' It's been going on for the last half hour – I don't think I want to know' she said.

Just then the door of the office opened and 2 or 3 men carried out someone who I can only describe as the remains of a tragic car accident. I heard one of the guys say 'He's still breathing shove him in the van. All I can remember then was this mound of bloodied mass being dragged across the floor and up the stairs, leaving a long red trail across the dance floor.

Val went to the office door and just stood there hand held over her mouth as though stifling a scream, I went to her and she pointed down at the floor, I saw an old wooden chair, strips of bloodied, ripped gaffa tape fastened to it, pieces of gaffa tape on the floor...and then...next to a pair of large bolt cutters i saw....2 fingers – oh my god i hoped that poor bloke didn't play the piano.

Within seconds both me and Val were ushered out back to the bar by a large muscle of a man, we sat quietly at the bar, numb and wary, the man shoved 2 very large glasses of Bells under our noses, 'Drink them girls' he ordered. We didn't need telling twice. Val turned to the man and said ' Can I have ice in mine' – balls of steel that girl.

MARLEY

If Marley had of been a spice girl – then he would of been 'Posh Spice' Immaculately pressed 'stones' trousers, black blazer, brilliant white 'Sherman' shirt, hair shaved every 2 weeks, smelled like a Parisian brothel, shiniest of shiniest black 'Brogues' . He adopted the nickname 'Marley the Coathanger' from the lads, this was because when he got lucky with the girls and he cashed in his 'favour' cards, whilst they removed their belly warmers and lay there patiently on the bed – he'd still be looking around the random bedrooms for a 'coathanger' to hang up his 'chinese laundered' clothes.

 No – the bedroom floor wasn't the right place for his immaculate attire.

 Marley teamed up with Robbie. Both good mates, he and Robbie were like two peas in a pod, and although they had quite a few admirers, they were both selective in choosing only, girls who wore apparel of the same quality and price range as theirs. They both married early on and had kids.

Marley ended up marrying one of our 'lot', Polly, great girl who could handle Marley enough to eventually tie the knot with him and still keep the creases in his 'Stones' razor sharp. Me and Nelly went to their wedding, I remember it well, Polly walked up the aisle in the church Face glowing with a massive smile on her face.

 I turned to Nelly and said ' She looks really happy' 'Yes she does' replied Nelly dryly ' That's because she's realised that she's given her last 'blow job' I was in fits of giggles, guests were turning round looking at us both, the more they looked the more we giggled, we just couldn't stop. They are still happily married to this day and after 40 years.. nothing's changed, he's still living in his 'Posh Spice' world and his designer labels Impeccably dressed in Armani and Louis Vuitton, and driving his snappy BMW. Well done buddy.

COL

Col, was another of my close pals, she bore an uncanny resemblance to 'Heather Lockyear' a very pretty and famous actress in the 70's, sparkling blue eyes and long blonde hair, Col, could twist the lads around her little finger, and very often did.

We had some great times, she was seeing one of the brothers David, they eventually got married, had kids, and after a few years of realising they'd made a mistake – they divorced.

When Col first started seeing David, I was seeing Tommy, we'd often go out as couples, but the best times we had, were 'after' our 'couples' night out.

The lads would walk us home, unknowingly, drop us off at the front door, then like two crazy caged polecats who'd just been released, we'd frantically change into our 'shades' or' Chelsea girl' clubbing gear, then straight out through the back door, into our waiting, pre-ordered taxi, and off to Boltons finest...

The Bees Knees club on Crompton way. Neither of the lads ever clocked on. Thank God !

Col, had a job for a short while in a local tablet factory – so our little nights of boogieing to Donna Summer were fuelled with an abundance of little happy popping pills, gratis of her unknowing employer.

One night, we'd both had one of the regular ' fall outs' with Tommy and David, The usual petty arguments over absolutely sod all - but hell hath no fury like a woman scorned..They had pissed us off... So we sat up in Col's bedroom, and we decided for a laugh we'd send them both letters pretending to be two hopeful love struck admirers, claiming they had fancied Tommy and Dave for ages.

We were both fully aware of the size of Tommy and David's ego's, and without any shadow of doubt, they would believe they were genuine letters.   After devising two great 'love' letters declaring our love and immense passion, to meet up with them both, we signed the letters separately, Col

signed as Fran Zovercote, I signed mine
Paula Zanarak.

Now even to the untrained brain of a
baboon, Reading them names out loud to
anyone would have been more than obvious
that it was a piss take, ie: Fran's Overcoat,
and Paula's Anorak, But, not them two, Vain,
Over egotistical sex hungry dim wits.

The fell hook line and sinker, The next night
me and Col, walked into the Market Inn,
Tommy and Dave were prancing about like
two pubescent, giddy schoolboys, Letters in
their hands, showing off the letters, and
telling all who would listen, about their two
mysterious, 'Continental' admirers.

 Then as they glimpsed us coming through
the doors, their voices instantly took on a
higher pitch, desperately hoping we would
take the bait and maybe just maybe show a
little spark interest and maybe feel a little
Jealous ? - No chance!....

That night our sides ached with laughing,
tears streamed down our faces leaving milky
white stripes on our ' Rimmel face make-up,

and... we wet our pants..true...It took a while for it to sink in to the lads that I was Paula and Col was Fran....It took even a little bit longer for them to see the funny side. And as most men do when they've been stitched up by a woman they arrogantly protested that they had known all along it was me and Col - what a pair of Pillocks !

MANNY ROAD AND FRED DICKY

A lot of Saturday afternoons were spent in the Market Inn or Wellington pub, a.k.a the 'Welly' watching sport on Grandstand.

However if there was a 'Home' match playing at the Wanderers they'd use the Market and Welly as a meeting place, and then after filling up with a few pints, The white army regiment of 20 to 30 'skins' would march down Market Street, and onto Manny Road heading for Burnden Park, all 'Tooled up' with their lead pipes, heavy duty mold grips, jemmy's and whatever else there was handy in their 'dads' toolbox

All wearing their blue and white striped neck huggers, ready to watch their idols kick the visiting teams arse, and even more ready for them to kick the opposing supporters arses if the 'Wanders should lose. This was one of the times when other neighbouring towns united together as an army, Tonge Moor, Horwich, Deane, Astley Bridge, Great Lever Daubhill all were one unit – However On non match days, this unity would be absolutely non-existent ,each town would fiercely protect their territory, and God help any trespasser who should visit, uninvited, unless they wanted a ride home in an ambulance. One of the main characters at the 'matches' was a more than 'handy' guy called Fred Dicky, nice enough bloke but took no shit from anyone, No one with an ounce of brains would ever challenge him.

I remember Fred spending some time as a doorman, at 'Troggs' But the main memory I have of him was, the home matches. You could hear Fred's stentorian voice all over the terraces...'Give em a zigger – Give em a zagger' the Lever enders would reply to this with a 'Zigger, Zagger, Zigger, Zagger Oi ! Oi! Oi!...sounds a bit naff now, but hearing all that massive crowds response – Now that was Unity. Fred's still a character in his home town of Bolton, still an avid Wanderers fan – and a fully fledged Northern soul Man – Keep the Faith Fred.

MAX

Max was another member of our girls squad, short black bobbed hair, chocolate brown smouldering eyes, figure to die for, Max had her own flat, me and Tommy would babysit for her on odd occasions, She'd go with friends to the 'Palais' nightclub in Town.

Max's flat was on Bolton Road, One big room, with a Couch, a toilet, a sink and a pull down from the wall bed. One night Max was out on the lash in Town.

Me and Tommy after settling the baby to sleep` were in the bed, lying there having a puff on the Park Drives after a session of doctors and nurses.

Suddenly there was a hammering on the door like a epileptic bailiff. Thinking it was Max, who could have forgotten her key, Tommy jumped out of bed, and grabbed the first thing to cover his well endowed, but very limp rhythm stick..

In them days us girls wore 'bra-slips' underneath our dresses, a sheer see through frilly piece of flimsy nylon, attached to a bra, Mine was lemon with a lace frilly hem and cleavage line.

The banging got louder and more urgent , Tommy without noticing, being more interested in covering up, grabbed the bra-slip and quickly pulled it on, just then the window to the flat violently burst into shattering pieces and from it emerged this guy holding a make shift Tarzan rope which he'd used to swing in on, from the outside building....For what seemed like ages we all stood there looking stunned and speechless.

 I stood there looking at Tommy, his 6' foot 3' solid frame, scantily clad in my little lemon number, me with my sari styled duvet cover wrapped around me and Tarzan standing there holding part of what looked like a washing line rope.

All hell broke loose,   ear bursting, effing and jeffing, and free for all physical interactions which gradually died down as Tarzan explained he was an old ex of Max's, He thought that Max was with another guy in the flat , Jealousy getting the better of him, he decided to use the old Farnworth ' If the doors locked find another entrance' way to face his assumed rival.

The baby unbelievably slept in her cot all through unharmed or disturbed.

 It took Tommy quite a while though to accept he had been caught with his 'pants down' so to speak, and his lemon bra-slip attire was a talking point for everyone in the Market Inn for many months after – obviously when he wasn't there.

THE SADDLE

The Saddle was another of our habitats, however it was used more by the 'older' Farnworth crew', Jimmy Kelly, Towny, Wally, Hassy, Plum, Ferdy, Davis, Tetley, Unni, Bri Goddard, Topsy and Polly wick , even neighbouring lads from Little Hulton were allowed to drink there without any aggro, Johnny Leyland, Pete Calderbank, Jimmy and Dicky Saville, Jimmy Rothwell were regulars, even Scouse a Boltonian would mingle in with the Farnworth lot, and though they didn't look for trouble – It always found them !

They would strut about in their Crombies, Two-Tones and Royals, they were an army in their own right – The Farnworth First regiment, they had no fear.

One of the lads, Jack, built like a British 'Challenger' Tank and just as hard was the 'Daddy' of the crew, he could handle his own 'business' and anyone elses at the same time, he took no prisoners.

One night me, Jack, and Nelly, were walking up to 'Smokey's' pub on higher Market Street to meet some of the others.   We were just passing the Number 8 bus stop, when off jumped 6-7 Bolton Lads.

The leader of this rampant beer fuelled crew was 'Clarky', known to everyone in most areas as a ' cowardly wannabe tough guy bully' who could only play games if he had his equally cowardly pack of cling-ons behind him, in search of any unlucky guy who had no back-up mates with him, and just for fun beat the shit out of them till they were almost lifeless.

Bang !! It happened so quick, all I remember is seeing Jack grab Clarky, by his Harrington Jacket lifting him up a good 2 foot from the ground and then like a Miami Dolphin quarter back he flung Clarky as you would a rag doll through the Bus shelter window, as Clarky lay stunned and bleeding on the floor, Jack looked at the other 7 lads and said 'Next'....not one of them moved, except to help Clarky to his feet who was completely dazed and unaware at what had just happened, Jack outstretched his arms and said ' NEXT ! No I didn't think so – daft twats'.

And just as though nothing had happened we three carried on to 'Smokey's' to meet the others.

MAD MARY

Mad Mary, as she is now known, was at one time one of the prettiest, kindest girls you could ever meet, I know this, because she was my elder sisters best friend and also her chief bridesmaid at her wedding. Mary was a little shy but loved life and was always smiling.

This all changed when she was in her late teens, both her parents were ultra strict Catholics, very religious and God fearing folk, she wouldn't ever dare miss church or holy days masses (and believe me there were many to attend) . So when Mary's Father died, her Mother possibly due to her grief at losing her husband, quickly became consumed and even more possessed with her religious beliefs, and demanded that Mary, followed her every command.

 Before and after school, Mary was ordered to Kneel and pray, constantly, every day in her kitchen, in them days the floors were mainly tiled and hard.

If her Mother ever caught her talking to any of her 'boy' classmates, Mary was punished severely, she would first be beaten with a large buckled leather belt, then made to kneel on a broom handle on the hard floor for hours on end, praying to God for her forgiveness.

It wasn't long before Mary's personality had changed, she became a withdrawn and frightened nervous wreck of a girl.

She began showing, manic behaviour, wild and apparently this gradually transcended into her normal behaviour, and she would often be

She was unaware that this behaviour was fuelling the warped minds of ruthless cruel classmates, neighbours and scandal mongers.   Soon venomous gossip exchanged amongst them and she was ridiculed and laughed at wherever she went.

She hid away most of the time, her Mother now completely in control of every breath and movement Mary made. Her cruelty had no bounds. This went on for many, many years until her Mother died.

 Sadly by now the damage done was irreparable, and now having to leave her home, for shopping and errands, everywhere she went she was hounded by schoolboys and girls, spitting on her, throwing stones and anything else they could find at her, following her around and calling her names.

On several occasions Mary was pushed and shoved and ridiculously tormented by these pubescent animals.

I'm not quite sure how, when or where, but Mary met a Man, called Colin (not his real name), to be honest I never liked him, he looked snidey and lecherous, but Mary seemed happy, she married him after a couple of years and all seemed well, then a couple of years later she became pregnant, I remember seeing her and talking with her at this time, and was amazed at how her 'weird' behaviour and constant nervous chuddering had mellowed, I thought this pregnancy had helped her calm down a little, and hoped it would continue.

However, soon after the little baby girl Sophie (not her real name) was born, we learned that Mary had, had the baby taken from her and put into adoption. The truth eventually emerged, it seemed Colin, had systematically beating Mary regularly, not only that he'd been tying her up to the bed and burning her with lit cigarettes, only untying her to feed or change the baby, she was terrified of him, her only concern was to protect Sophie. He was a savage brute.

Soon the Farnworth 'jungle drums' where beating and it soon became the local talking point that Mary had, had all her house windows smashed with bricks from her neighbours, It was alleged that Colin had been grooming and having sex with young schoolgirls in the area, after plying them with drink and cigarettes, he was a paedophile a filthy nonce. Colin got taken away, was charged and sent to prison whilst Mary lived in her own prison in Farnworth, constantly pointed at and abused by the social 'know it all's' – Mary had no clue about Colin or the indecent behaviour he had been involved with, she was locked away in the bedroom most days but she paid highly for his sick behaviour, and she lost her beautiful little girl.

Since that day her mental ability and behaviour deteriorated drastically, Her solo public outbursts of rage and vile language became a common occurrence, and people, would avoid her, Mary stopped caring, the system stopped caring, she had no one.

I still see Mary conversing with herself and arguing with her shopping trolley when i go up Farnworth sometimes, and I try to have a chat, She easily remembers all my families birthdays and goes regularly to the Church to light candles for people she knows who have passed away, I know she never lets a day go by without thoughts of Sophie, who will now be approaching her late thirties.

God Bless You Mary – You were Dealt a bad hand in life.

4 WEEKS LATER..

Tommy stood leaning on the roof of his 'borrowed for the day' Zephyr car, He drew on his Park Drive fag, his eyes squinting in the hot August sunlight, he looked around him, bare derelict land facing a huge brick wall topped with barbed wire, and a tall hangman's tower, he didn't want to be here.

He'd been here a few times before – only at the other side of the huge wall, too many memories. He bent down and picked up a piece of red house brick, launching it at a large brown rat a few yards away, nibbling away at an old chip tray, the rat scarpered.

Tommy looked down at his watch and then leaned into the back of the car through the window, pulling out a can of Tetley's bitter. It was warm – but wet.

A large door in the castle style wall opened, three men came out all clutching small brown paper bags.

Two of the men proceeded to a nearby Red Datsun car, the third man cantered over in Tommy's direction.

'Alright Tommy mate' said the man with a familiar smirk Tommy last saw 4 weeks ago...'Yeh I'm good Pete' said Tommy as he handed over a can of the warm ale to him.

Both men stood there for a minute taking in the moment, then wrapping arms around each other shoulders they had what can only be described as a 'man hug'. But soon realised a handshake would have been more appropriate and separated in an embarrassed scuffle.

The journey back to Farnworth from Strangeways was pretty quiet, Tommy knew from his own experience that Pete needed to get acclimatised to his permanent release and to gather his thoughts.

Pulling up into Pete's Mums drive, The lads sat there, for a minute, smoking their half spent fags and drinking the last dregs of their cans.

'So when did you get this car Tommy?'
asked Pete with a grin.

'It's not mine Pete – I've borrowed it' replied
Tommy. 'Does the person you borrowed it
from know ?' asked Pete.

'No – Does he fuck' said Tommy.

And with that Pete got out the car and into
welcomed outstretched arms of his Mother
who was now standing at the front door.

'You coming in for a brew Tommy? She said.

'No Thanks Mrs Lionels – Things to do' said
Tommy. And he left.

LAST CHANCE HOTEL

Pete sat down at the dinner table, with his Mum, Dad, and Brad.

Mrs Lionels placed down a huge plate of Homemade 'Tater Pie' with red cabbage and mushy Peas in front of him – Pete's favourite.

The food wasn't on the plate very long, and it was then followed by a large helping of Apple Pie and thick yellow 'birds' custard – also Pete's favourite – Pete stretched back on the dining room chair – full and complete.

'Thanks Mum' said Pete, The tea was lovely – you're the best 'tater pie' maker ever' and he gave her the 'thumbs up' sign.

'Right Peter' said Mrs Lionels sit yourself down on the couch, I'll go and wash these pots up and then I'll fill you in about all what you've missed while you've been away.

Pete sheepishly looked up ' Sorry Mum – I've got to go out tonight – Things to do – people to see – we can do it another night'

'Oh Peter, you've only been home a few hours, cant it wait' said Mrs Lionels with a huge sigh. 'No Sorry Mum it can't wait' said Pete getting up from the table and heading towards the stairs and up to his bedroom to get changed.

Mrs Lionels shook her head, in acceptance, but what she really wanted to say was ' You'd better not be going out looking for trouble – she knew Peter only too well, this wasn't his first homecoming, and probably knew it wouldn't be his last.

Pete sat on his bed, he pulled out his polished 'ox blood' Doc Martens from under it – his 'bovver boots' as they were then known. Changing into his Levi Jeans, Black granddad shirt, he laced up the boots – ready for the night.

Grabbing a Dark Green Harrington Jacket from the coat hook at the bottom of the stairs he shouted ' See you later Mum – Don't wait up'

And he was gone.

It was Friday night, the Market Inn was buzzing, everyone patting Pete's back, and offering to buy him a pint as he came through the doors. 'Save it for later' Pete said as he walked to the tap room.

Popping his head round the door of the room, he scanned around the tables for Tommy, he caught Tommy's eye 'You ready mate' he said. Tommy nodded downed his last bit of Tetley's and picked up a large black plastic bin bag which didn't disguise its contents very well. They both walked out of the Market Inn and onto the Car Park at the back.

Like a pair of praying mantis they scoured the vehicles for their ride. After little debate they chose a cream Ford Cortina, and after a couple of minutes of fiddling about, they were in and heading down the road to....The White Horse.

'Ferret about ?' they asked Malc the barman

'Not been in here for a couple of weeks now' Malc replied ' I heard he's drinking in the

Greyhound now on Bolton Road' 'Cheers bud' said Pete and they were off.

The Greyhound Pub was a isolated part of Bolton Road no man's land between Farnworth and Great Lever, didn't get many punters just the stalwart regulars. As Tommy and Pete walked in heads turned, everyone knew Tommy and Pete, and they knew they weren't there to join the darts team.

'Ferret' questioned Tommy looking around at the silent faces. Few of them looked back at their drinks and shuffled their feet under the table. Old Harry sat in the corner looked up from his pint and gazed over the bar into the direction of the other room. Both Tommy and Pete followed the lead. Ferret propped up the bar watching the little portable telly perched on the optic shelves.

Tommy and Pete stood by him like a bloodhound round a fox, Ferret turned slowly, NO escape. Before Ferret could stutter a word, they had both frog marched him from the pub and into the back seat of the Cortina – No one in that pub uttered a word.

Ferret sat in the back of the car speechless with fear, Tommy, went to the boot, pulled the black bin bag and threw it on the back seat next to Ferret. 'Just going for a little ride Pal' said Pete 'Make yourself comfortable'

Ferret opened the plastic bin bag though he probably already knew what was inside, a garden spade..his lips trembled and he begin to ramble, jabbering ,whimpering and sobbing sentences that were inaudible.

The drive took about 20 minutes, Belmont was pretty quiet at that time of night, the only witnesses would be sheep.

'Please Pete, I'm sorry, I'll get your money, I promise, Tommy don't do this Please – I'll get you the cash tomorrow honest i will'

'Shut the fuck up' came Pete's reply.

Dragging Ferret from the car who was now in a Crazy frenzied state, brought on by complete terror. Tommy threw the spade at

Ferret 'DIG!' he commanded, Ferret curled up like a foetus on the slutchy earth, Please God, Please don't do this he screamed – his cries for help went unnoticed, He knew he was digging his own 'resting place'. Pete grabbed him and pulled him to his feet ' You heard the man – DIG!' Ferret grasped the spade handle, his legs turning to jelly and no chance of making a run for it..he slowly dug the earth..Tommy and Pete looked on completely emotionless. 'No one takes the piss out of me' said Pete. After an hour or so Ferret still whimpering and begging to go home. His grey Slazenger tracky bottoms were now completely covered in his own Faeces and Urine, Tommy took the spade from Ferret, 'Fucking filthy dirty bastards shit himself' said Pete 'Strip them filthy clothes off Ferret' Ferret by now in a state of complete desperation and surrender, did what Pete said. He stood there amongst the fir trees and brambles shivering and without dignity.

Smack !! Pete brought the spade down across Ferrets back, he buckled and fell to the ground.

And with a few hefty bodily contacts with the 'Doc's' Pete made sure Ferret would never attempt to step over the mark again. Pete picked up the bin bag and pulled out a large polythene 'body bag' , Ferret now in a semi conscious state put up no defence as Pete and Tommy bundled him in the bag sealing up the zip and then placing him the boot of the car. They drove for a good hour or so until pulling onto the motorway hard shoulder. Pulling ferret from the boot they dragged his half dead body onto the third lane. 'See you Ferret' said Pete, 'come and have a beer with me when or IF you ever make it back to Farnworth.

They both then got in the car and drove home.

No one ever heard or saw Ferret again for several years, then he was sighted on the Blackpool Sea front working as a bingo caller for one of the amusement arcades.

MR FIX-IT

I first met Andy who was also known as Mr Fix-It shortly after I'd left school, He got his Fix-It name from a large logo of a hypodermic needle and the words 'MR FIX-IT' tattooed on his right arm.

He was for a short time seeing a school pal of mine, Suzanne. I'd gone to Troggs, and she was there with him, Tommy at the time was having a four month stint in Strangeways – for borrowing cars.

Mr Fix-It who I'll call Andy for reasons that will soon become clear, was tall blonde smartly dressed and wasn't bad looking.

After that I'd see him around and about Farnworth, mainly in Troggs, we'd chat and became friends, at the time I was hanging round with 2 other of my friends Helen and Viv. We were good friends with the one of the original owners of Troggs – Charlie, he was pretty old (to us anyway) and he'd often give us free promotional tickets for 'Blightys' a larger more prominent club in Farnworth, that always had star acts on.

Charlie was a lovely guy and one night he told us that he was brining in some free tickets for us for the 'Drifters' so to be in Troggs the next night to collect them as he had left them at home that night.

We were there next night, only No Charlie ? Not giving his absence much thought we were surprised later on that night, to see 'Andy' giving out a few of these tickets to some of our crowd, he said Charlie had given them to him, Strange – we didn't realise Charlie was that good a friend to Andy ?? We also noticed that Andy was wearing a watch very similar to the one Charlie always wore, noticeable because it was an obvious expensive one and also had, the same unusual strap like Charlie's.

Andy also was buying drinks for everyone, we did think it a little weird, but didn't think much of it, until the following night at Troggs when two of Charlie's partners came down, we knew them quite well, and we asked about Charlie.

They took us to one side and explained that Charlie had been found dead 2 days ago in his home, there was a Police investigation pending, there had been a break-in, he had been hit with something heavy, and the shock had given him a heart attack and killed him. We all three stood there speechless and numb, and all thinking the same thoughts !

Now, remembering what we did after that sounds absolutely crazy, but none the less we still did it.

The night after Me, Helen and Viv were In Brackley street, next to the Market stalls and about a hundred yards away from Troggs, one of our 'lads' Dave Wakerley was looking for Andy and he wasn't too happy – Andy had allegedly broke into his Mum and Dad's house on Cross Street, and robbed them, broke into the gas meter and picked up some jewellery belonging to Dave's Mum, he'd heard that Andy was in Troggs and was going down to 'have a word' with him and anything else he needed to do, Dave was fuming mad. For some reason we thought it was a good idea to telephone Troggs (there was a pay phone at the bottom of the entrance door) and ask for Andy to come to the phone. This we did and Andy answered. 'Hello Andy' I said trying to disguise my voice in what resulted in a cross between a menopausal wild woman and an Austrian Yodeller. 'We know what you did to Charlie' I rambled on 'You robbed him and stole the Free tickets for Blighty's – You killed him Andy !!. Yes we displayed really silly, stupid and completely childish behaviour.

 The phone went dead – I'll never know how within 30 seconds of that call Andy appeared on Brackley Street carrying a large hatchet (which we assumed he had picked up from the cloakroom in Troggs which had been kept there for the last couple of years – no idea why or for what purpose.

He came charging at us, his face was blue with rage, and has he approached us we scattered among the empty Market stalls. 'Come here you bitches – I want to talk to you !!' he spit. Not a prayer, we ran like Red Rum through them stalls, and yet for some reason we thought if we went over to Troggs we'd be safe ?? .

Half an hour later we watched the doors open and Andy walked in – The strangest thing was he was calm and unruffled, and, after getting himself a pint he casually walked over to us, I don't know whether it was nerves knowing, that our 'Farnworth Lads' weren't there to give us backing but all three of us sat there smiling, not sure of what was going to happen next. Even stranger Andy returned our smiles and said 'Now girls were the Fuck did you get that crazy idea from about Charlie ?'.

'We made stupid excuses and pretended that we had just been winding him up, after we saw him giving out the tickets the night after Charlie's death. 'Alright ladies, no harm done' he said 'But let's not play these silly games any more eh? Could create some Big problems for you all' We never did mention it again (up until now) Fear played a large part in our silence.

We didn't see Andy for several months after that night. We put it down to him lying low, knowing Dave was after ripping his arms off, as were several others who we learned he had robbed.

G.U.S GIRLS

I was 14 when I met Tommy, I'd just left
school, St.Gregory's in Harrowby street. My
first job was working at Burtons Sewing
factory on Worsley Road, sewing Men's coat
bottom linings into the jackets, the wages
were pitiful, I earned 6.50 a week, gave my
Mum a fiver of that for my keep, I was left
with 1.50 for working 40 hours a week,
sheer slavery – I hated it! It didn't last too
long, and soon I was back on the 'Dole'
looking for work. I decided to go to College
at Victoria Road in Horwich and here I got a
few decent qualifications, which opened the
doors for my employment with a large office
- G.U.S, (Great Universal Stores) a catalogue
Company near Orlando Bridge in Bolton.
This was the happiest time of my life,
eventually working my way over a short time
to become a 'line head 'or a glorified
supervisor. I trained new staff how to input
information or data into computers and
would regularly travel (all expenses paid) to
sister company's in Manchester, Chorley,
Oldham and Preston, the wages after

expenses for travelling, training and anything else I could put down for expenses were fantastic – I learned to live the life I thought I was born for.

I had two sets of Friends, my Farnworth Pals, and my G.U.S pals in Bolton. I loved my life. When Tommy was having his breaks at Haverigg Prison or Strangeways, I'd spend most weekends with the G.U.S girls, Julie Greenhalgh, Sue Hamer, Barbara Fogg, Barbara Yeats, Joan Greenhalgh, Joan Isherwood, Anne Hackey. We would rampage through Bolton town centre every Friday night after being paid, first stop hen and Chicks, Brandy and Babycham then Red Lion for Stella Artois, Old Man and Scythe for the Scrumpy Cider, and Yates wine lodge for the Australian white wine which was lethal, rocket fuel.

Our stomach linings were made of lead. These days, I only need to sniff a glass of Baileys for an hangover.

There was always an abundance of Footballers, or execs always ready to splash their cash. I was always faithful to Tommy, but like any other red blooded female I liked a flirt, and there were some fit guys out there, I was faithful but....... I wasn't dead !

SO HERE IT IS MERRY CHRISTMAS..

'Our lot' spent many Christmas's together, there was always a party at someone's house or flat. We were always respectful and made sure our cigarettes were put out before we dropped them on the carpet, our empty cans were always stacked up like a pyramid at the side of the sink, and any condoms placed carefully in an Asda bag at the side of the bed.

We would drink dynamite cocktails, smoke Lebanese gold and eat space cakes, there's a popular saying – 'one life – live it' and we certainly did. We had no Filters.

We'd sit in the Market Inn or Welly – juke box on full blast and we'd a belt out the choruses to Slade, Wizard, The Pogues, Christmas offerings , in unison, regardless of whether we knew the words or not.

New Year was the best, Gordon the landlord of the 'Market 'would always make sure 'our lads' had a few free pints, me Nell and Col also had a few glasses of 'snakebite' on the house' That would be Gordon's Insurance that we would make sure there was no trouble, and if there was – we would 'sort it.

But there never was.

Well except for one occasion, We were all sat in the Market, Boxing Day it was, doing the usual, drinking, chilling, and sharing a few spliffs. In walks Robbie, the room quickly went silent, Robbie stood there a huge gash across his forehead, blood streaming from his nose and lips, a big blue swelling around his eye, his clothes were covered in slutch and blood, and his 'crombie' was beyond repair.

'What the fuck happened to you?' said Tommy helping him to a seat. Robbie, wiping his face with a bar towel explained that he had just left Julie at the bus stop near The Flying Shuttle Pub, up Highfield (Area bordering Little Hulton via a bridge) when 4 lads had jumped him, said he was in their territory, and to tell his 'lot' that's what they can expect if they overstep the line. Mick knew the ringleader – a big ugly mother F***** called 'Rat' . Tommy and Pete said nothing, just drank their pints and with David, Marley, Brad, Mick Bull and Megs left the Market.

They knew where they were going, and what they had to do. But first of all, on the way there they called at Tommy's flat in Newbury, to pick up an item that would be useful. 'Here Brad – keep hold of that' said Tommy.

Tommy and Pete walked into the Flying Shuttle, heads turned and within seconds the four skanks had emerged and were ready for battle. 'Take it outside lads' said the burly landlord. And they did, and the cowardly, skanks were greeted with a battle they wished they had never began, as the rest of the crew performed their ambush, bottles bricks anything that was lying around to hand were used. The 'Rat' was left for Tommy - Yes 'Rat' was his ! Tommy didn't take any prisoners and 'Rat' looked like he'd done 10 rounds with Mike Tyson when Tommy had finished. The other 'skanks' all ran but 'Rat' stayed in Tommy's possession.

At the back of the Flying Shuttle, there were some houses being built, there were planks of wood and debris lying about everywhere, It was here that Tommy thought it a good place to get his useful 'Hilti Gun' from Brad, and whilst a couple of the crew held 'Rat' down he calmly, nailed the battered hands of 'Rat' to some scaffolding planks, but not before he had made 'Rat' remove his coat. 'Tell your 'lot' that's what you get if you overstep 'MY' line. They all returned back to the Market Inn. Robbie still sat there, 'Here you are Robbie' said Tommy ' Try this on for size' and he threw over the 'Crombie' that had once belonged to Rat.

DOWN THE BROW

Stoneclough Brow was, and still is a long winding road from Farnworth and neighbouring Kearsley eventually leading to Prestoleigh. Down towards the bottom of the brow was 'Prestoleigh Working Men's Club' another of our haunts on a Monday night, here we'd all congregate and as usual drink, dance and put 'our' world to rights.

The Prestoleigh 'lot' would merge in with the Farnworth 'lot' - Mick Greenhalgh, Steve Jennings, Phil D, Malcolm Sutcliffe 'Sucki', John Derbyshire, and Rob Garner were just a few of the names I remember. We all shared our likes and dislikes of the same rival neighbouring towns.

'The 'Working Men's' was a great place to let off steam, It stood on its own, on some land at the back of The 'Grapes' pub. In hot summer nights we'd all congregate outside the club drinking cold beers and potent snakebite (mixture of bitter and cider – although nowadays the bitter has been replaced with lager).

It was on one of these nights, Tommy and Pete had a bit of a 'set to'. There had recently been a little bad blood between Tommy and Brad, Pete's brother, for a few days, over some Money dispute, Tommy tried to deal with it 'Tommy's' way but Pete didn't agree – Brad was his brother..So this black cloud loomed over the two and they wisely kept their distance, however both turned up at the 'Working Men's' this Monday night. The atmosphere was pretty dark and eruptive.

When Tommy and Pete collected their beers from either end of the bar and walked outside, everybody including the bar staff followed onto the front field -

For a minute or two both stood there like 2 gunfighters at the O.K corral, Pete put his Pint down, Tommy handed his to me.

Now slowly approaching each other. 'One shot, each Tommy' said Pete ' You first' said Tommy –' make it a good one!' at that Pete swung out with his mighty hammer of a fist and landed it straight on Tommy's jaw line. Tommy stumbled back felt his face and then he too hammered his fist at the side of Pete's head. The two both clearly, punch drunk wavered about on the dry grass under their feet. 'It's done' said Pete and with that they both stumbled towards each other and shook hands. Tommy smiled 'You broke my jaw you wanker !' 'You bursted my fucking ear drum' said Pete and they both walked back into the club, followed by the 80-90 punters who felt like they'd been robbed of their anticipated 10 rounds or knockout Mayweather major boxing event.

WHO'S THE DADDY..

Most of us girls, kept to our own group, now and then we'd allow one or two 'stragglers' or 'hanger onners' to join us on our nights out, One of the girls, Ivy, was the female equivalent to Brian, she loved the lads, especially if they were someone else's,- ours!!

She would always be found out, and then dealt with accordingly, but where there's no sense there's no feeling and she always managed to slyly edge her way back into our circle. She knew that she was hated by everyone of us, girls - Hated by us, but enjoyed by the lads – regularly, whenever it took their fancy. Strangely the lads always got forgiven for their 'romps' with Ivy.

One particular time 'Poison Ivy' as we called her had been up to her old tricks and whilst us girls were on a Blackpool weekend trip she was left to her own devises and had a field day, one night bedding three brothers, alternately. One of our girls Sue was gutted, Ivy had slam dunked her fella, Sue had just got engaged to him and now any future they were planning was on the scrap heap.

It was a couple of weeks later when Ivy slithered into the Market Inn with an equally renowned slapper friend, unaffected by the verbal abuse and threats she was thrown by us all at the top end of the room.

After half an hour or so she and the friend went to the toilets, Ivy had left her bag on the table. Quicker than lightening, Col bolted towards the cheap plastic bag and rummaged through it, producing 6-7 Johnny's – or known today as condoms, Ivy was well known to be prepared for whoever or when ever, carrying condoms in her bag was just as necessary as carrying lip gloss. without much thought 'our' girl had removed a brooch from her dress and proceeded to prick an hole in every packet.

'That should teach the slag' said Col, all of us now in fits of giggles. Ivy returned and looked at our smirking faces of satisfaction nervous and wary of what was going on.

She drank her beer and left without a look in our direction as she passed.

The incident had been completely forgot – until 3-4 months later we saw signs of a swollen bump under her C & A's weather worn smock coat, she was pregnant ! Now thinking back it was an evil thing to do – but hey – let's not worry too much about the past.

Her son still lives in Farnworth, I often wonder to myself - out of all the Farnworth lads she must have slept with.......

'Who's the Daddy'.

P.C FRED RATCLIFFE A 'PROPER COPPER'

Most of the coppers at the Farnworth cop shop were as bent as a nine bob note, they were either uniformed thugs licensed to batter any drunken misfit that was unfortunately picked up by them in the 'black mariah' on Saturday night, or in liaison with local burglars and robbers, some even had a wish list for items they wanted, often turning a 'blind eye' or losing bogus charge sheets after they had received their, 'Ferguson Videostar' recorder, or Atari games console, even the odd bit of Jewellery was considered.

However there was one or two of them who were decent coppers, they were fair and treated the Farnworth lads with decency and respect. Which earned them respect back in return from the lads. P.C Fred Ratcliffe was one of these 'good cops' He never battered, blackmailed or talked down to any of the lads, and the lads highly respected him, He would rather try to guide them on the path of 'straight and narrow' – rather than guide them to the path of Risley Remand Centre.

One time Tommy and one of his long time buddy, Murphy were 'on a job' at the back of 'Quicksave' on Longcauseway, they'd persuaded one of the night staff 'Roundy' to pass boxes of Quality Street, cartons of Foxes biscuits and a few cases of Scotch whiskey over the wall, the last box was just being passed over, 'Well Done Tommy lad, almost got away with it this time' said an amused P.C Ratcliffe shining his big flashlight onto the faces of the caught pair. 'Pass them back right now, you pair of pillocks – as for you Murphy, you've missed a meeting with Billy Allsop, your probation officer for this ! – Pair of useless prats the both of you'. He stood and watched Tommy and Murphy begrudgingly pass the merchandise back over the wall to a stunned 'Roundy'.

When the job was done, P.C Ratcliffe strode over to Tommy and whacked him across the back of his head. 'Now go home the pair of you before I pull you both in – next time if I catch you there will be No get out of jail free card !'

Tommy and Murphy did just that, thankful it was Fred on duty that night and not any of the other P.C knob heads.

Sadly Fred died several years ago – but he certainly was the true definition of a ...proper copper. R.I.P Fred

THE PIE PLACE

A lot of the Farnworth crew, at some time or other worked at a local small pudding and pie factory.   Your job was either a 'Hot-pot lidder' a 'Pudding filler' or a Packer, I worked there as a packer for a few weeks in between my college course and my G.U.S days.

Joan was an hefty 16 stone 'pudding filler' she sat at the end of a conveyor belt filling suet filled pudding cases with meat from a long tube stuck inside a large tub of minced meat and onions, which was placed by the side of her.

 Joan was slightly mentally challenged and spent most of her time, eyeing up the young lads that worked near her, or making lewd comments about what she'd like to do to them given half a chance, the thing was Joan had top and bottom dentures, and as she spoke both top and bottom would battle with epic proportions and rattle like a monkeys cage, often falling out into the meat and onion mix. This was not a problem, Joan would delve into the elbow deep mixture and rummage around for her lost mixture swishing away in the warm swill until she recovered her pearly whites – which were now brown and slimy, none the less Joan quickly rammed them unwiped back into her open orifice. What a Star.

From that day on I've never looked at another pudding or pie with the same gusto as I would a chip barmcake.

PARKS & RECREATIONS

As you are already now probably aware,
most of us spent our time in the 70's & 80's
drinking, snakebites, cherry B's and cider, or
Pints of Beer, The cost of a pint in them days
were 10 pence for Mild, 12 Pence for bitter,
and 11 Pence for mixed).

Cigarettes weren't a mortgage payment
then, and we'd smoke Consulate, Park Drive,
No.6, No.10 or whatever we could get away
with buying in the local shops.

Some of us would have a cheeky spliff, of Leb
Gold, Red Leb, Grass, Cannabis, Weed, Bush
etc, some many different names, all did
more or less the same thing, made us feel
'Big' and helped us 'chill out.

The more knowledgeable and regular, Wigan
Casino, Va-Va, Nocturne, Maxwell Plums,and
Uncle Toms Cabin members of 'all nighters'
would use Duramine, Pondrax, Tenuate
Dospan, Double Parelli's and Barbituates,

Blueies, etc.. We knew most of the Phartmacetical terms for them. Most of these were a form of 'Speed' and would be used as a 'keeper upper' when needed, which was most weekends. Common names used for these were, Whizz, Billy, or Paste.

The more qualified 'drug squaddies' would use heavier shit, Sniffing Cocaine (Coke) from a rolled up 'tenner', or Crack, a crystal 'Rock' a form of Cocaine usually in a pinkish, yellow or white powder form which could be smoked, Both offered a short but intense high – temporarily speeding up the way your mind and body work. Crack was the most addictive.

LSD or 'Acid' was a powerful 'psychedelic hallucinogenic drug, we had 'happy' names for these tiny little pills, 'Strawberry Fields' , 'White Lightening' and 'Purple Haze'.

This tiny pill could change your hearing, or view of objects, Lamposts could turn into giant ear-wigs or caterpillars, calling out your name, Colour infused flower petals would rain down from the sky and change into goldfish , you would hear music from a Harp, played by Father Time as he sailed up Market Street on his Peter Pan Galleon Ship.

There were many names for this tiny atom of a tablet, Blotters, Smilies, Micro dots, Trip, Rainbow, Lucy (Remember the 'Beatles' hit Lucy in the sky with Diamonds).

There were some of the more habitual users who had probably gone past the point of caring what drug they used, or that they had used so many in the past they were now content to rely on 'Barbiturates' or 'Barbs', our lot stood well clear of these, the users – AND the drugs, The barbs would act as a central nerve depressant and could produce a wide spectrum of effects, from mild sedation to total anesthesia, they were originally prescribed for anxiety, sleeplessness and stress. Most regular users would experience a 'downer' when the drug began to wear off, this could, and often did result in severe forms of temper outbursts and violence, usually with innocent bystanders, the users unaware of the situation after they had woken from their state, sometimes days later.

I remember several of our 'older end users and abusers' finally losing their battle to stay alive,

Their 'before they used' and 'after they used' mental photos I still have of them are unbelievably impossible to imagine they could ever have be the same people.

MA BAKER

Kath Blaine or 'Ma Baker' as she was known to many, moved to Farnworth from Bolton, she was a 2-3 years older than us girls and never really interacted with our group. I didn't like her much, and I made sure that any conversations that may of occurred between us was, short and to the point.

Her lifestyle didn't and wouldn't ever fit in with our group.

Kath, was an attractive blonde girl, who was confident, ruthless, and made certain that her presence was acknowledged , wherever she was.

She fitted into the 'Barbs' group of our Town, regular visitor to a 'druggie house' in Central Farnworth, where she and her cronies would 'crash out' on a tatty mattress thrown onto the empty living room floor, after one of their 'crack' or 'barb' sessions.

Over a couple of years, she became a fully fledged dealer and bulk supplier of 'illegal' substances.

If she had any filters, they were invisible, she trusted no-one, gradually her 'line of work', took her further afield, Liverpool, Leeds and eventually to Cardiff, It was here she nested for a while hiding low from other and 'bigger' dealers.   She had made many enemies by now, often caused by her lack of interest in paying for her supplies.

At some stage they eventually caught up with her and she was found naked bludgeoned to death in her bath tub, The killer was eventually caught, Jailed for his crime, only to be let out of prison 15 years later to kill someone else.

THE RETURN OF MR FIX-IT

Apart from a small number of my close friends, this is the first time I have openly been able to speak about this.

Mr Fix-It or Andy, if you remember my earlier chapter, turned out to be not the nice guy as I'd originally thought, when I first met him, but a Vile, much hated, vicious drug abusing thief.

But then there was another string he eventually added to his bow

Tommy was on another of his six month breaks (usually lasting only four months for good behaviour) at Her Majesty's pleasure.

It was a Saturday afternoon and there was an 'all dayer' scheduled at Troggs, which would merge into an 'all nighter' there.

I'd gone down to see my pal Val, and another girl called Pat who had moved to Farnworth from Wigan, she was living in a

Flat on Ivanhoe Street – We named her 'Flat-Pat' as there were several of the girls named Pat, Stoneclough Pat, Fat Pat, and 'Pat the Mat' and this stopped confusion.

Everyone felt sorry for Flat Pat, she had been thrown out of her home in Wigan by her Mother who had moved in her new boyfriend, the pair didn't get on – and so someone had to go – and the boyfriend won.

When we first met her, she had been given a bar job at Troggs, she knew no-one, had no friends, very little cash, not much food, and a sparse bin bag of clothing.

She was relying solely on the little handout she received from the DHSS until she got her first wage packet.

Quite a few of us took her under our wings, and would give her clothes and buy her suppers when she worked at the bar.

So, now back to Troggs.....I walked in 'Alright Val' I said. Val turned and smiled, looking a little flustered, 'Whats's up' I asked, 'Trying to get everything sorted out in time for this 'all-dayer' Flat Pat's late, she should have been here an hour ago – so I'm left doing her work – and mine' she replied.

'She'll be here – don't worry, she needs the money' I said as I collected glasses and bottles from the tables, from the previous night and put them on the bar.

I stayed a little longer giving Val a hand with the room, and helping her finish of the dregs from the almost empty whiskey optics.

Still no sign of Flat Pat.

'I'll tell you what I'll nip down to her flat and see if she's O.K' I said.

It's strange how some events in your life leave simple non-meaningful memories, I remember that day I was wearing a white cheesecloth smock top with a high ruffled neckline, a pair of navy blue flared pants with white pin stripes, and a pair of Navy blue and white double wedged 'clog' style sandals.

I set off for Pat's Flat, on the way I called at Hanburys supermarket in Brackley Street to pick up a few items of food for Flat Pat's empty cupboard. I bought a bottle of Milk, a loaf, six eggs, packet of ginger nuts, jar of coffee, a couple bags of crisps and a tin of Spam.

I reached the gate of the basement flat, knocking loudly on the paint deprived shabby front door, no response, so i banged loudly on the front bay window room hidden by rusty metal venetian blinds.

I saw the blind move up a little and seconds later the door opened. 'What the hell are you doing here' I croaked, nervously hoping Flat Pat was somewhere behind in the entrance hall.   'Nice to see you too' he sarcastically grinned, come in 'Pat won't be long she's just gone to the shop for me some fags.

It was – Andy !!

I followed him down the dark hallway and into Pats Flat, there was a make shift bed on the couch, where apparently Andy had slept the night.

'I've come to see why she's not gone in work, and I've brought her a few bits and pieces for her cupboard' I said feeling his eyes following me into her kitchen as I unloaded the bag onto the kitchen unit side.

'What you doing here anyway?' I asked. How the hell did he know Pat?

'I met her when I was coming out of the chippy the other night, after she was coming home from her shift at Troggs, we got talking, she was immediately attracted to my charms and good looks, so I walked her home, We both got on like an house on fire, and she asked me in for a brew, she knew she was onto a 'good thing' with me and Ive been here since that night' he slyly grimaced.

Ignoring the fact that he was now right behind me in the kitchen I began putting the food into the top cupboard. 'I think I'll make a 'butty' he said and picking up the tin of Spam he said 'My favourite this – I love Spam' - unbeknown to me at that time, he wasn't referring to the tin I had just purchased for Pat, but this was his sick terminology for his deprived needs.

I nervously walked out of the kitchen 'How long she going to be' I asked.

'How long is a piece of string' Andy replied with a strange menacing rasp. And he sat down on the make shift bed.

'How's my mate Tommy doing?' he asked 'Or should I say 'Who? Is my mate Tommy doing?' he laughed 'Is he looking after your needs – or do you want to me to show you how a real man makes you happy ?

Ignoring his latter comments, and wishing I had the nerve to swing my right Derba clad clog in the centre of his nether regions. 'Tommy's fine – I'm meeting him later this afternoon' I lied.

Now I was aware of Andy's sickly trance like stare. 'So he's not sat alone in his little Strangeways cell playing with himself, thinking about what he want's to do to you when he gets out ??'

'Fuck off Andy' I hissed. 'Now don't be like that, I thought me and you were friends, come and sit here on the couch' he ordered, his glassy staring eyes now watery and wild. I refused saying I had to leave, but my excuses went on deaf ears, Andy grabbed my arm and pulled me violently down beside him, kneeling over the top of me he began nuzzling at my neck, thinking now I remember the slimy wetness of his slaver.

I tried to push him off, but my efforts only seemed to make him even more determined, I screamed at him that Pat would be home any minute, he laughed 'She's gone over to her Mum's in Wigan – so we've got a little playtime before she gets back!'

Somehow I managed to scream out for help, but in an instance I felt Andy's fists hammering down on my head, at some point I think I passed out, but not before I felt Andy viciously ripping down my Navy blue flares, and then reign some more punches down on my head and face. I've no idea how long this went on for but, on coming round I saw Andy stood up over me now fastening the zipper on his jeans.

He realised I was coming round, and he smiled, 'You alright ? bet your feeling better now you've had a 'good seeing to'

 Andy had raped me.

Sitting up on the couch I was afraid to move or speak, scared of encouraging to continue with his brutal his attack.

'Now that's done, how about we have a brew' he said, he seemed unaware or oblivious to what had just happened. I shook my head, 'I need to go now' I said.

'O.K' he agreed, 'Thanks for dropping by, and offering me your services, I might bump into you in Troggs, one night.

My mind went immediately back to the night on the Market when Charlie was killed, and how he had changed from a raging psychopath, wielding a hatchet, to a more refined and calm state when he entered Troggs half an hour later. He was an animal.

Did he regret what he'd just done – NO!
Did he show any remorse for his evil actions
– N0! Andy was a law to himself.

I got up to leave, and as I did Andy grabbed
my arm ' Now lets not make a big thing
about this, I won't breathe a word to anyone
about it, and I know you wouldn't want
Tommy to find out about your little naughty
escapade, and what you get up to when he's
not here' he said.

 I trembled I just needed to get out of that
room.   'Remember I'll always be here for
you if you need me again' he smiled
threateningly 'But If you feel the need to 'lie'
about what 'really' happened – well I'm sure
people will be asking – just what, you were
doing in a flat alone with a guy – especially
when they learn your 'boyfriend is in
Strangeways, Just like me, they could be
thinking you're probably missing a bit of the
'old Saturday night takeaway' and you've
come to me to give you one – so to speak'

he said as he cruelly laughed at his off hand and what he thought was funny comment. 'So, let's not rock the boat and cause any unnecessary problems – especially while Tommy's banged up – Fuck!! it would drive him stir crazy ! So let's think of today as our little bit of fun' he said

I pulled my arm away and walked as fast as my jellified legs would permit.

Once out on the Street, I inhaled a deep breath, and then, immediately bursting into tears, had this just really happened?

 An old woman was sweeping her path in the next garden, she looked away when I walked past.

 I can't remember the walk home, or how long it took me. When I got there I went upstairs to my room, I needed to think.

Head exploding, I wiped the blood stained trickle coming from my nose, and changed my blood stained underwear.

I sat in the bath, now hurting from top to toe, my cheek bone was turning into a large purple bruise and my head was covered in lumps.

In them days, rape wasn't something you could just report to the Police, there was numerous statements and enquiries, fully executed examinations, There was no DNA and any accused rapist was allowed to walk on the streets until actual evidence was found and justified.

The biggest fear I had was Tommy finding out, mainly because I hadn't even had sex with Tommy then, We'd been together 18 months, a lot of them months Tommy had spent inside, I was brought up in a pretty strict Catholic household, sex wasn't an easy option in my relationship, and as much as

Tommy tried, I wanted to wait until I felt the time was right – I thought about the name he used for me - 'Tin Knickers'

My main worry was, would Tommy believe my real reasons for going to Pat's flat, would anybody ?? I soon began doubting myself – did I encourage him? Did I bring all this onto myself ? - the answer was NO!!

I decided to say nothing to anyone about it and somehow, over the next few weeks, I managed to subconsciously train my brain into thinking it had happened to someone else.

I was then, oblivious as to how my mind had been irrepairably damaged.

When Tommy was released – I was uncertain as how I'd react on seeing him, would I burst into floods of tears and blurt everything out?

Unbelievably on Tommys release, when I met him and was strangely calm and sedate. I said nothing about what had happened.

We went down the Market Inn that night and carried on as normal. Nelly and Brad, Col and Dave were all there, Nelly came over 'Bet your glad he's home' she said. I smiled and nodded. Nelly gave me a concerned look, she'd been noticing over the last few weeks I'd been looking strained and washed out, and constantly asked if i was alright or needed to talk about anything. I explained that It was lack of sleep and extra overtime at work, she put it down to missing Tommy. If only I could have told her just really what was wrong, but I was scared she would tell Brad, and Brad would tell Tommy.

On the way home Tommy tried to convince me to go back up to his flat and spend the night with him, feelings of panic emerged like tidal wave, I think I used every excuse under the sun to get out of going. Tommy gave up, annoyed and frustrated by my constant refusals to sleep with him. This quickly erupted into one of our usual topical arguments, I loved Tommy and up until several weeks ago, I'd decided that it was time to 'bite the bullet' and stay over at his flat, when he came home from prison, now though things had changed, I'd changed, I was scared and frightened at how he would react if he ever found out, would he look at me differently, would he think it was my fault what had happened? I didn't know – and at that time didn't want to know. Realising I could now no longer justify my refusals, I decided 'call it a day' finish our relationship.

Tommy took it bad, but like any other self consumed skinhead of the 70's pretended to his friends that he didn't care, 'There's plenty more fish in the sea' he'd boast. And for a time he went all out fishing !

More weeks went by, I still went to the local hang-outs, not so much the Market Inn, Nowadays, it was mostly couples, something I no longer was. I spent more time with my two mates Viv and Helen, we'd go to Highfield Youth Club, Nevada in Bolton, house parties and Troggs, sometimes I'd see Tommy watching over from his corner of the room, turning away when he caught my eye.

One night in Troggs with Viv and Helen, I saw Tommy come in with the usual crowd, I also noticed that clinging to his arm, was a scruffy auburn haired pretentious acne infected sweaty trout of a girl, laughing, looking round for approval at her 'newly' acquired arm piece. Typical slapper who obviously wore separate post code on the bottoms of her shoes. Blood ran to my head like a burst geyser. I knew her – she knew me, She knew that I'd broke up with Tommy, first hand from me. It was only the week before she was telling me in the Troggs toilets, how sorry she was, that we had broke up and that how she thought we were made for each other – Bitch ! Viv watched my glare 'Here drink this cock calm down – ignore her' she said, she knew there wasn't an echo of a chance that I would. As the night got longer, my temper got shorter.

Last orders, we all marched towards the exit doors, The trout was right next to me, on seeing me she said ' Oh hi, Alanah, didn't see you in here tonight' (fucking liar!!) 'Love your dress' she rambled on 'Thanks' I replied and the geyser blew ! without any hesitation I smacked her with a punch that even Mike Tyson would have been proud of !! – It didn't stop there I can't remember my next actions only that they had to be a good mix of 'Chuck Norris and a Japanese suicide bomber. Next I was being carried outside, lengthways by two hefty doormen (bouncers) still kicking and punching- well above my weight.

Tommy came out to me. 'What the fuck has got into you' he angrily asked. 'Not You' I screamed back, 'Don't expect me to play my part – if you're auditioning sloppy seconds for my role !!' and walked on my way.

I was walking home, still raging, to myself thinking about how that trollop would dare walk into 'our' club with 'my' boyfriend and then having the nerve and audacity to compliment me on my dress – fucking slapper!! It was made even worse by the fact that she already knew me and Tommy, fully aware that it was an unspoken rule amongst us that no other girl should try walking in another girls shoes with her boyfriend (ex or not).

I was now walking up Harrowby street, I could hear voices shouting my name, turning round I saw Helen and Viv panting for breath behind me. 'Hang on, wait for us' they called. I stopped and waited till they caught up. 'Bloodyhell Alanah' you nearly knocked her into the middle of next week. Next time I thought, If there is one – maybe I'll do just that !

I was just coming towards the corner turning in the direction of my house, Val lived here in the corner house. And just as Helen and Viv caught me up a taxi pulled up at the side of us, out got Val. 'You O.K Alanah' she asked. 'I'm fine thanks' I replied.

In fact No!! I wasn't fine I was angry, upset, I was gutted without warning tears streamed down my face like an Himalayan waterfall, the events tonight and the deep hidden stress and upset from weeks before all forged together now, my shield was down and I sobbed like I'd never be able to stop.

'Come on, come inside for a brew' Val offered fumbling in her bag for the keys to her front door. We all four trundled inside, Val lived alone with her Dad, who worked night shifts, so her house was empty but for the four of us.

We sat in the little front room of the terraced house, Val made some coffee, whilst Helen and Viv sat either side of me on the sofa both their arms around my shoulders. I don't know whether it was the sympathy and support I was getting, the relief of letting go of the past frustrations, the fact I'd seen Tommy with someone in my place – Self pity ? I hadn't a clue, but the tears came stronger and faster.

After a while or so I'd calmed down Val had brought us some Coffee and a plate of digestive biscuits.

I knew now that I couldn't keep it in any longer and through spasms of sobs I explained what had happened in Ivanhoe Street to my three trusted friends.

The room stayed silent throughout my recollection, I could see that Val and Viv were shocked and upset by my story, Helen looked angry 'That bastard can't get away with this - Tommy needs to know' she said.

'No' I argued, 'It's too late to tell him now, he'll think it was my fault.' I begged and pleaded with the three, not to tell anyone, I was ashamed. We all eventually left for our own homes in the early hours of the morning, I managed to sleep right through to the following afternoon.

It was no longer a secret – although the weight on my shoulders now a felt a little lighter, The deep emptiness in my gut was still there.

The week flew past, and it was Friday night again, Trogg night, Me, Helen and Viv met at the usual place we always met – Farnworth Bus station.

We were sat at the bar in Troggs, chatting with Val who was working, we'd all had a good few glasses of Snakebite, followed with a few more whiskey chasers, I felt a little easier. I knew Andy wouldn't be anywhere in the area, he would now have heard that Tommy was out of prison, and besides, Dave Wakerley still needed a few words with him. Andy was only brave to defenceless women not Men!

I was sat with my back to the door 'Not speaking Tommy' said Helen as she spotted him being served at the bar behind me. 'Alright Helen, Alright Viv, see you've both brought your psycho mate out with you again? Said Tommy as he nodded in my direction.

'And I See you've NOT brought your skanky slapper out with you' said Viv pleased with her quick retort.

Tommy took a sip of his Tetleys and moved over to his corner.

Later on that night, a few of the 'Stoneclough lot' came in, one in particular who I had known from school, Phil, he was a couple of years older than, and he came over for a chat, he was a nice lad, good looking, and was a massive fan of David Bowie. Phil would copy the outrageous 'Bowie' fashion style clothing, he always looked good.

Phil made me laugh, and I sat most of the night just chatting with him, Even missing a few dances on the dance floor with Helen and Viv.

One of the downsides of being Tommy's girlfriend, was that no matter where I went, there was always one or two of his crew a few yards away, watching my every move, ensuring, I behaved myself and that any uninvited presence was quickly warned off, or manually helped away.

'Where the fuck were these morons when I needed help weeks ago ?

God help anyone should come dancing with me on the Dance floor – Like Phil did that night. It was the 'last dance' both physically – and literally ! – and as a Bowie number 'Starman' played , Tommy stood at the edge of the D.J stand staring like a crazed Sioux Indian who'd just selected their prize scalp.

I'd had a few drinks by now and couldn't care less what Tommy thought, and carried on till the end. Suddenly without warning one of the lads head butted Phil onto the floor, I stood there as I watched blood stream from Phil's face, shocked and bewildered at what had just happened and why ?

I sobered up in a flash. I should have known – you 'Tossers' I spat at the lads, who stood there looking down at Phil 'Don't touch what's not yours' said Brad 'Stay your distance now Pal' said Megs. At that moment I hated the lot of them. Tommy included.

Two or three weeks had now passed, Me and Tommy where still on bad terms, if any one of us ended up in the same watering hole, one would leave.

Except one night in the Market, The weather was bad, it was pelting it down outside, Me Helen and Viv walked in the back room, there sat Tommy with Pete and the lads from Warburtons bakery, deeply engrossed into a game of Poker.

There was no way we were going back out into that weather so we got our drinks and sat down – I sat on a stool with my back to Tommy, but I could feel his eyes burning through me from behind.

We'd been in half an hour when Dave Wakerley and Murphy walked in.

Giving their usual greetings, 'Alright Tommy, Alright Pete, who's winning?' they both asked. Pete looked up with his sneaky sneak look and said 'Who do you think?'

The 'Warby's lads regularly lost half their wages and sometimes more to Tommy and Pete – they had their own personal system – It was called 'Cheating' An extra ace here, an odd Queen there, a wink, a tap, even the way they smoked their fags was sign language to them two. No one could ever break their codes.

'Hey you heard about Andy ******' said Murphy 'Only gone and got himself banged up for a few years for raping a 14 year old kid in one of the Fairground 'kip trucks' – It's in the News of the World, Bastard battered her first then left her there crying, one of the Fairground lads found her. A few of the 'gaff' lads went looking for him, but he'd done one, taking with him the weeks takings from the toffee apple stall. She was only the daughter, of one of the coppers at Bolton Nick, anyway he was picked up somewhere on Halliwell Road, in a betting shop, bet he got a fucking good slapping in them cells before he appeared in court'.

'Lucky I didn't get my hands on the thieving Bastard first said Dave Wakerly, he'd have got more than a good slapping.

I sat there frozen to my seat, Helen and Viv just sat staring, not knowing what to say to me or do whilst Tommy was there.

I'd had a couple of Ciders, and within seconds both had come back bringing with them the fish and mushy peas ,I'd eaten for my tea earlier, I'd spewed my entire stomach contents over the Pub table. I got up and flew from the pub, leaving my two buddies sat there to explain the explosive mess to Gordon the Landlord.

To this day I don't know how the subject of Ivanoe Street come up, but Helen and Viv said that after I'd left, Tommy started coming out with cutting comments about my behaviour over the last few weeks, so they both decided to tell him the real reason why our relationship had ended.

I was told that after they had told Tommy, he just sat there in the Market Inn for the rest of the night in silence, with Pete, and that they both didn't leave until the early hours of the following morning.

That following Monday, I'd just got off the bus from work at the Bottom of Glynne Street. Robbie stood there, I nodded 'What you doing down here' I asked. 'Come to see you' he said 'Tommy wants to talk – he's over there parked in that Purple Zephyr' he said pointing in the direction of the back street of the Shakespeare pub. 'Ha, another of his 'borrowed cars ...'Nothing to talk about' I snapped, 'Well Tommy thinks there is' he replied 'Just ten minutes – that's all' ......and, Tommy bought the car from Dave Jolley, so its ligit, except that its got no tax or Insurance...

I walked over to the car, got in and sat there, so did Tommy for what seemed like an age.

Eventually, 'Why didn't you tell me' he said.

I looked around at the brown tortoise shell dashboard and scruffy cream leather trimmings, not really knowing how to respond, Tommy seemed calm – for now.

' I don't know' I stammered. 'I didn't think you'd believe me' and with that once again I burst into tears, thinking of that horrible afternoon, and remembering the brutal punches of Andy's fist banging on my head.

Tommy pulled me to him 'Stupid – that's what you are fucking stupid!' and he held me tight, I felt safe and secure and realised everything would be alright.

The next hour or so was spent gradually re-living that day, I explained why I'd gone to the flat and what Andy had said to me after.

Poor Robbie was still stood on the corner waiting, when I emerged from the car, he smiled and gave me the 'thumbs up' 'Sorted' he said and I smiled.

That night I had the best sleep I had, had for the last 3 months, hopefully my nightmares and sleepless nights would now come to an end – But not for Andy – his were only just beginning.

Me and Tommy were once again back as a couple, but it took a while for me to forget the slapper he'd brought with him to Troggs that night, and every opportunity I got I'd have a dig at her and his poor taste ' I didn't shag her that night' he said ' I sent her home – told her she was surplus to requirements – that was good enough for me. Never saw her again in Farnworth, lucky her.

I obviously, knew that, the next time I went into the Market Inn, everyone would be aware of what had happened, I remember walking in with Tommy, nervous and apprehensive of how people would now see me and their reactions. I didn't need to worry, walking in that night I was greeted by Nelly, who couldn't wait to tell me she was pregnant, Col sat there with David 'Are we sorted for the Bee's Knees next Saturday night' she whispered, making sure it was out of Daves radar, Robbie had a nice big double whiskey sat on the table with my name on it, Pete, patted the space next to him ' Come and sit here sweetheart – I've kept your seat warm. Even little Karen sat in the corner – sneaked in by Brad had a hug for me – Yes, these were my mates, they never once doubted me, I'll never forget that night.

AND SO...THE FINAL CHAPTER

The weeks passed, everything seemed back to normal, then one night we were in the Welly, One of the lads, Bernie Pearson walked in 'There's been a few calls for you in the Market tonight' he said to Tommy 'Cheers mate' said Tommy and not long after that we were all marching back up to the Market Inn.

Roughly about an hour later, Gordon popped his head round the door to the back room 'Call for you Tommy' he said, Tommy went to the phone, after a few minutes he come back in the room sat next to me put his arm round me and whispered in my ear 'It's sorted now love'. I hadn't a clue what he meant but thought it had something to do with the phone call, for some strange reason I didn't question him about it.

It was a couple of days later when I was in work, I got called to the office, I had a phone call from Val. 'Don't know if you already know, but I've just heard from one of my mates whose hubby is doing a bit of time in Strangeways, that 2 nights ago one of the other inmates was taken to 'intensive care', he'd been given a hot tub bath, by the other inmates, they had held him down submerged in one of the tin baths they use, in the shower room and filled it with Boiling water, apparently his screams could be heard as far as Lower Broughton, weird that the screws didn't hear him' she said sarcastically, anyway he's been shipped off to the Prison hospital, he's going to need skin grafts and be hospitalised for a long time, bloody painful eh? Poor Andy.

'Thanks Val' I said – see you on Friday.

DEFINATELY THE FINAL CHAPTER

My 'Definite' final chapter, now returns back to 2017.

Me and Tommy eventually ended up getting married, having 2 lovely children, Sherri-Lee and Jonathan, who the gave us three wonderful grandchildren, Kai, Max and Isabelle.

Our life together had its ups and downs (as does every marriage) but we survived everything that was thrown at us for 43 years. Sadly Tommy passed away in 2015, with prostrate cancer, leaving a huge void in all our lives, but also some incredible memories.

Robbie and Dave also sadly have now passed away.

Nelly and Bren (oops sorry! typing error) are very happily married and living in Wales with their lovely daughter, and their beautiful grandchildren. Me and Nelly (a.k.a Lisa Nelson once upon a time) are, and will always be, close friends, We still keep in touch and meet up at least once a year, reminiscing about our crazy but never to be forgotten youth.

Pete now lives close by and we still chat regularly on the Phone or he calls round, and brings me a meat pie for my dinner. He's such a charming, kind man, slightly different now, from the Pete of the past, as I once knew him.

Murphy still the ladies man, now an avid biker kitted out in his leathers and living the life with his 'patient' partner Dolly.

Max is now livingin Australia, happily married and regularly 'coming home' with Michael, her husband – you can take the girl out of Farnworth – but you can't take Farnworth out of the girl.

Harvey and Pauline (ohhh no, another typing error) are still happily married with grandchildren.   Not sure whether he ever did manage to get a BJ again though.

My buddy, Woody (a.k.a Billy Isherwood) Is I think ? living in his 'drum' somewhere near Tenby, he too has wrote a book 'Dead Man Walking' which Ive read two or three times over.

Col is still living in Farnworth, and we are still friends, and have shared one or two nights over a bottle of Wine and for an encore once again 'wet' ourselves when we remember Paula's Anorak and Frans Overcoat.

Viv, well she now lives in Chorley happily in a relationship with Dave Wakerley, we keep in touch, mainly through social media, but I'm sure we will have a get together before long. Helen, well she seems to have vanished from the face of the earth, but we may meet up again, I never say never!

Val, my lovely friend, who now lives in the Ulverston, It's only in the last few months we have got back in touch, but years can't or ever will take away our deep friendship.

My life has never been perfect – but who has ever had, or even wants the perfect life ? Memories are made through living, laughing and sharing the good times with the bad, regardless of the outcome, taking chances, making bad decisions, doing things we wished we had never done, been to places we should never of gone, but then if we hadn't – would we have turned out the same? and would our friendships have made such an impact on our lives ? I don't think so – and you know what ? I wouldn't change a single thing.

THE LAST CALL

Ive mentioned lots of my 'Farnworth' and 'Bolton' friends in my book, but theres many more that come to mind so just in case you ever buy my book...thank you for being part of my life .....

Bobby Hinsley, Phil Haslam, Graham Marsh, Ian Lightbown, Phil Townsend, Brian and David Heathcote, Lisa Nelson,Bren ONeill, Jimmy Rothwell, Brian Davies, Jimmy Kelly, David Whittle, Paul Sutty,Mick Walsh, Karen Plaice, David Sparks, Carol Nelson, Sue Boothsman, Mick Bullis, Alan McGregor, Mick and Les Robinson, Julie Walsham, Lil Rothwell, Paul and Howard Wilky, Bev Wilky, Maxine Cartwright, Fred Dicky, Richard Moffat (Scouse), Harvey Clugstone, Pauline Burke, Hilary Clugstone, Karen Rimmer, Mel Fleming, Gary Roscoe, Bernie and Pey Pearson, Kathleen Alker, Malcolm Sutcliffe, Steve Jennings, Mick Greenhalgh, Rob Garner, Karen Rimmer, Val Rigby, Tony

Walton, Baz Hindley, Glen, Harry, and Paul Worthington, Brian Goddard, Brian Howarth, Stan Berry, Anne Blower, Cathy Gatfield, Anne Collinson, Claire and Teresa Dowd, Angela Flitcroft, Freda Burrows, Bev Diggle, Tony Round, Jimmy and Dicky Saville, Lynne Hough, Dave Howard, Glenn Roberts, Johnny Leyland, Martin Curry, Karen Moores, Lil Rothwell, Jimmy and Gary Murphy, Dave and Phil Wakerley,Helen Pollitt, John and George Unsworth, Phil Dawsey, Billy Hardman, Jack Cartwright, Mark Aldred, Jean and Dawn Moreland, Arney Brown, Albert Howarth, Pete and Angie Calderbank, Jimmy Wright, Belinda Lomax, Stephen Barber, Stephen Whittlestone,Margaret Barnes, Judith Rothell, Brenda Berry, Angela Smith,Barbara Isherwood,Kieth McNeil, The Shaw brothers,Michael Toppy (Topsy), Ferdy, Tetley,Dave Jolley, Belinda Battle, Kenny McGregor,Brian Howarth... and once again........Thank You

23304980R00085

Printed in Poland
by Amazon Fulfillment
Poland Sp. z o.o., Wrocław